"After he drove man out, he place of Eden, cherubim and a flaming sword ˌᵤₛₕᵢₙg ᵦₐcₖ ₐₙₑ ᵢₒₙ ₐᵢ ᵤ g the way to the tree of life."

Genesis 3:24

"I can't go back. I don't know how it works."

The Wizard of Oz

This book is dedicated to my wife Claudia, companion, counselor, and best friend through the journey of life.

Jeremiah 29:11

ACKNOWLEDGEMENTS:

Thanks to Penny Winter, my sister, for her editing and helpful comments throughout. To my recovery brothers, especially Jerry and Michael, my sponsor, and their constant wisdom, strength and hope. To my old friends Peter, Paul and Bill, who have shared their weaknesses and struggles with me and listened to mine in return. To Bryan, Jon, Roger and Tim who share life with me every Tuesday and the Thursday men's Bible study at Church of the Redeemer, Jacksonville. To our children John, Lydia and Hope, who reflect bright rays of hope in a dark world.

Thanks to Ralph Heim for the poem "Disturb Us, O Lord." I am Indebted to Frank Lake and Robert Gaudino, who taught me to listen and ask questions and to my early mentors in the faith, Whitey Haugan, Herb Wagemaker, Peter Moore and Peter Rodgers.

Cover Art: Adam and Eve Driven Out of Eden by Paul Gustave Dore

DISTURB US, O LORD

by Sir Francis Drake

(Written after he had sailed around the world)

Disturb us, O Lord,

when we are too well pleased with ourselves
when our dreams have come true
because we have dreamed too little;
when we have arrived in safety
because we sailed too close to the shore.

Disturb us, O Lord,
when with the abundance of things we possess
we have lost our thirst for the Water of Life
when having fallen in love with time,
we cease to dream of eternity;
and in our efforts to build a new earth,
have allowed our vision for the New Heaven to grow dim.

Stir us, O Lord,
to dare more boldly,
to venture on wider seas,
where storms shall show Thy mastery,
when losing sight of land we shall find the stars.
In the name of Him
who pushed back the horizons of our hopes
and invited the brave to follow him.

Amen

ISBN: 1-4680-1633-4
ISBN-13: 978-1-4680-1633-8

INTRODUCTION

My father died January 16, 2009. The experience of walking through his dying process awakened my soul as nothing beforehand. Having not written a poem since I was seventeen, I now could not stop.

The aging process brings loss. Some losses are necessary ones like death, children leaving the nest, and health problems. Other losses are due to our wandering from the path of Christ and the consequences that follow. I have experienced both. Along with these experiences comes the feeling that things can never go back to the way they once were. We can only move forward, never backward.

The theme of the poems in this volume is a simple truth: it is only through the suffering, death and resurrection of Jesus Christ that our pain and problems, so deeply rooted in the past, can be both redeemed and understood. St. Gregory of Nazianzus in the 4th century said, referring to Christ, "what is not assumed is not redeemed," meaning that Christ had to take on our entire humanity, apart from sin, in order to redeem us. This also means that he experienced every temptation common to man. (Hebrews 4:15)

Thus Christ not only died for our sins by taking our place; He also suffered and died to transform our difficulties, weaknesses and problems both into ministries to others (2 Corinthians 1:3-7) and into our own highest joy. (Hebrews 12:2). Instead of weakness being a liability for ministry, Jesus makes it a requirement. (2 Corinthians 12:9-10)

These poems are about my struggle to learn this abiding, transformative truth: the deeper the mine, the more precious the gold. My prayer is for us all to recognize that the present joy we experience is a direct result of the suffering we have endured under his watchful, redeeming care and love. The human truth is that loss is unavoidable. But the higher truth is that nothing is lost to God, because if we allow him access to our souls, he will transform and use it all, to the benefit of others and ourselves, and ultimately for his glory.

(Note: The personal pronoun referring to God as "he," "you" or "him" is not capitalized in this volume. No offense is intended.)

TABLE OF CONTENTS

POEMS OF LIFE

A WORLD WITHOUT PRAYER

At that time, men began to call on the name of the Lord. Gen. 4:26b

These words fairly leapt out at me from the page as I read them recently. I had not registered their presence in the Bible before. They describe a time in the early days of man's creation when a great cataclysm had broken upon the world. Before the fall, man had dwelt securely with God in the garden provided for him. Man's relationship with God was one of implicit intimacy, where God "walked in the garden in the cool of the day" (Gen. 3:8) and where he spoke directly to Adam and Eve. (Gen 3:9-13). But after the fall, man's life became deeply troubled. Strife, murder, back-breaking work and troubles in child-birth and child-rearing became the norm, not the exception. Literature en mass from Milton's **Paradise Lost** to the present have described man's experience "after the fall." This is the world in which we now live. **However, it is not the world to which we are headed.** Even now the world "groans" (Romans 8:22-23) because we can see the new world that is coming, though we do not yet possess it. The gap between promise and possession is real.

The greatest and most enduring reality after the fall was Adam and Eve's loss of intimacy with God. The garden was the place they had lived with God. Now a "flaming sword" (Gen. 3:24) barred their return to that place of divine-human contact. They had to learn to cope in their new world outside the garden. Now you would think that prayer would have been their instinctive response to their plight. But no. We read that no one prayed. **No one.** Whether it was just too hard to pray, whether they were overwhelmed by guilt and separation, or prayer had not even occurred to them, we do not know. What we do know is that years went by. In fact, decades went by **before anyone prayed.** Genesis tells us that it was not until Adam and Eve's grandson Enosh was born that "men began to call on the name of the Lord." (4:26) Perhaps the new hope delivered with the birth of a grandchild was the catalyst to bring the first family back into relationship with God. The Scripture hints but does not tell us plainly.

There have been times of prayerlessness that have swept the west throughout history. We can think of Anglican rationalism settling over the dusty churches of England after the Enlightenment, or the rampant alcoholism of pre-Great Awakening America that gripped the country in the wake of Puritan decline, where it was said that half of America's 12 year old boys were alcoholics. The half-century assault on prayer in public schools certainly does not help our children to become people of prayer. The list goes on. People experience prayerless seasons for countless reasons.

What then drives a family, people, a country and a culture back to prayer? Trouble certainly does and our country is as troubled now as it has been during my adult life-time. But trouble can pass and with it the needs that drove us to prayer. No, there is a greater motivator for prayer than even trouble. It is hope. Perhaps Adam and Eve felt renewed hope that their grandchild Enosh might live in a better world and this hope drove them to prayer. But even this kind of hope based in family legacy is not enough. The world our descendents occupy may not be better and may be worse. History oscillates and there are no guarantees.

No, what drives us to prayer is the belief that our relationship with God makes all the difference, both in this world and the next. When those first humans began to pray they did so with the belief that "all was not lost." They had to deal with the world as it is, while at the same time believing that God had not abandoned them. But the "eternal hope" had not yet been purchased for the ancients.

We have far greater reason to pray. Our legacy and treasure purchased with the death and resurrection of Jesus Christ is surpassingly great, a possession unimaginable to Adam and Eve. The gift of God is nothing less than the truth that through the cross and resurrection we are a people of destiny, participants in the building of a "new heaven and a new earth." (Rev. 21:1) This is the "eternal hope" expressed so well in Romans 5:1-5 and Romans 8:22-25. Prayer is therefore redemption believed and applied, expressed in hope. It is the one thing a prayerless world needs most. The Christian message is simple. There may be no way back to the garden but there is a much better way forward to a promised, permanent yet unimaginable destiny. As Bishop Martyn Minns has put it, "We are all lost. We are all loved. We will all be transformed."

My personal prayer for you, as you read and meditate on the poems that follow, is that you will find rekindled hope and faith in the one who brought you this far, the one who will also lead you home.

Jay Haug
Ponte Vedra Beach, Florida
Winter 2012

POEMS OF
DEATH AND
RESURRECTION

AS HE LAY DYING

Our father died last month,
His earthly life
Fading as the setting sun,
Sacred in its glowing serenity,
Life's day quietly closing.

But was some new day
Being born,
Unseen by bedside family?
He dreamed of unopened gifts,
Meetings with unstated purpose.

But now, look!
He saw something, his eyes fixed with wonder
In the upper corner of his room.
No more conversation, just beholding after
"I think I'm dying."

But in the dying
Someone was coming
For him, just for him.
Right on schedule
As if appointed by a Higher Authority.

No more talking.
His earthly presence is fading
Even as the new day breaks upon him.
Our unworthy eyes cannot see its dawning,
Only the quiet sunset as he is taken by the hand.

His few words are noted, recorded, treasured.
"Are all the bills paid? Yes, Dad, don't worry."
The biggest was paid long ago
On a wooden cross, with agony, for him
Resurrection now his to live in everlasting day.

BOOKENDS OF LIFE

Dad was born in July heat,
Philadelphia summer, 1918.
The year of the great
Influenza epidemic
The end of World War I

He died in the dead
Of winter
January cold, 2009
The beginning
Of a new presidency

While attending his Maine memorial,
In Florida, the yellow hibiscus
In our front yard
Died from the cold.
I will cut it back

It will live again
Despite the severity
Of the cold and pruning.
Against its dead appearance
Life will emerge again

So will his.
As the deadwood
Of his fragile body is removed
And his glorious body is revealed
Unseen by unworthy human eyes.

Bookends
Set the beginning and the end
Of our human story.
They cannot comprehend or bracket
The eternal now of those beyond our reach.

FILLING HIS SHOES

Dad died two weeks ago
But his clothes live on
In this world.
I wear them
In various states of newness.

When we are gone
Our clothes are useless
But the earthly travelers
With unspoken inner respect
Don our shoes, using up the tread

I now understand more fully
"To walk in his shoes"
Sometimes his socks too.
How did he feel when he walked?
Were they as comfortable on him as me?

Perhaps there is part of him
That could rise up into my feet
Through the leather.
If it is possible
I want that.

The other day I found his handkerchief
In the pocket
Of the bathrobe he left me
I don't use handkerchiefs
But I will wash this one and use it.

One day, all of his things
Will wear out.
So will I.
And I will join him
In the place where nothing does.

APOSTOLIC TREASURE

Meditations on the Burial of My Father

Kittery Point Maine

July 17, 2009

In death
God waits upon the living.
To what end?

To remember Dad
To treasure his ways, his voice
The memories and thoughts of him
That steal upon us in mid-summer days
Making us smile and cry together.

The empty chair, the undisturbed bed,
The unspoken greeting
Yes, and more
God waits upon us.
For what?

To believe. To raise the flag in the morning breeze.
To go down to the cove
Where the lost sell drugs
And steal moorings
Because they have none for their souls.

To paint gold leaf on crosses,
High and lifted up
So wayward sons
Can find their way home.
Dad and God call us.

To sit in our own chairs,
Uninterrupted, to ponder eternity

And tell one lost and starving soul
What we have seen and heard.

The world is lost. Christ its only Captain.
It's compass guiding to safe harbor.
The only Anchor
In the raging storms of life.
The apostolic treasure.

Yes, God waits. Dad waits.
People in need await.
God's eyes and Dad's are upon us.
Here is the treasure.
Ready to be spent.

WHEN GRIEF CAME TO STAY

Grief came to stay
One day
Not the searing, shocking stab
Of sudden loss
But the quiet presence of worldly absence.

This feeling of losing Dad
After so many long years
Is like welcoming a new family member.
Knocking at my door, he asks,
"May I come to stay with you?"

I dare not deny him entry
For he comes with truth
And precious reality, the kind many flee from.
Life ends. Dad's loss now the wallpaper,
The background of routine days and nights.

Sometimes my friend takes center stage, bringing tears
Other times , he says
"Let me just sit here with you"
Or "I'll remain over here in the corner
Til we can visit again."

He is patient and unobtrusive, my quiet friend
One day he will be smaller than today
But he will never leave, this side of paradise.
He carries gifts of loss and memory
I receive instinctively each day.

Fond memories flood my mind
Warm days long ago
Of home and hearth

Dad's sandpaper cheeks I kissed before he died,
Morning sea lapping boat hulls,
Chores, trips and quiet advice.

I want grief to stay
We are now friends wherever life's journey leads
My guide, until that fatherly reunion
Replaces fading remembrance.
Then we will talk of the intervening years
With tears of joy and knowing laughter.

On that day, my friend tells me
His work will be done.
He will disappear like mist in sudden sunshine
Eclipsed, no longer needed
But for now I cannot live without him.

TIME AND MEMORY
(Of My Father's Death)

Is memory distorted
Or clarified as time goes on?
Is it my mind and emotions
Painting evocative pictures,
More about me than him? I wonder.

No more can he "think anew and act anew."
His deeds and words done and said
Complete and catalogued this side of heaven.
Nothing can be added.
Nothing subtracted.

Lately, I would tell him stories
Of my childhood
He had told to me, then forgotten he had told them.
It is odd what we remember
And happen to forget.

That voice
He said your name, then paused.
You waited for the observation or question.
Well thought out, pointed
Spoken evenly and calmly.

His words were few
Commanding attention
Tasks to be completed… "Tomorrow, could you help me to…"
Politics, religion, history…family memories
"I've never heard that story before."
Silence…
"Tell us the story about…"

I understand hagiography now
Washington and Lincoln carried into heaven by angels
Exalted tributes. But no.
Give me human, concrete memories beyond distortion,
Surveying lands, splitting rails
Valley Forge cold and jokes
Told around pot-bellied stoves in county seats.

Resurrection stories,
In their simplicity, endured.
Eating fish by the seashore,
Walking to Emmaus, hungry people eating bread,
Touching his wounds.
On the Damascus Road, sad women…
Dawn at the tomb.
"Cast your net on the right side of the boat…"
"Did not our hearts burn within us…"

It is not the exalted state
We crave, yes, will to remember.
No. It is the common, the routine,
Even the wasted moment
Remembered in tranquility.
That can never be exalted
And thus distorted.

They say when the saints die
Their last look and vision
Is not toward transfiguration, clouds, the exalted state.
But they see the dusty walk to the cross,
A crown of thorns,
Rejection, bloody cries and sins forgiven,
That God became a man.

HANDS OUTSTRETCHED

Newly born, his hands
Wave in the air,
Grasping, muscles starting to form,
Preparing for play and work,
Not ready to grasp the nails for carpentry.

Growing, they run over the pages
Of his Father's Word,
Circling and returning again
They point to familiar phrases,
Truths held in remembrance, necessary for Life.

In Jerusalem, lost to his parents
But not to God,
He raises gentle and inquisitive hands,
Disputing with the elders-
"Did you not know…"

As Messiah, he launches out with hands of healing,
Touching the eyes, raising Jairus's daughter, "talitha cumi"
The man born blind, receiving the spittle,
Upraised hands stretched toward Lazarus's tomb,
Fingers writing on the ground, "neither do I condemn you."

Teaching hands that embrace hearts and minds
On the mount twixt heaven and earth…blessed are you…
He points, invites, welcomes, imparts hope, loves, uplifts.
Asleep, deep into the night, the hands of God
Rest motionless in quiet, only to awake the dawn.

Confronted by the religious, his hands remain at side,
Calm, yet firm, resolute, determined.
Until finally when night falls,
With friends, after his hands
Unhurriedly wash their feet,

He gives them bread and wine (himself).

Now the hands are taken, jerked behind,
And bound with ropes, he is forced away.
Hands raised again and tied to the flogging post,
And flexing to the pain and evil of the world
Full force reins down upon his back.

Finally, the hands of God are stretched
One last time, upon a plank on the ground
Nailed by another who holds the hammer he once did.
Receiving blows, taking the darkness upon himself,
Outstretched hands raised on hardwood of the cross.

At last, his hands, now limp, unclasp themselves in death
With a final cry, they release because nothing is left to hold.
"It is finished." his hands now accomplished all their work.
Today, our work still comes from his hands, as does the invitation
To serve him with our own.

MICHELANGELO'S PIETA

Slowly, carefully, hand over hand
His body lowered down
From the cross.
Mary reaches toward him,
Not knowing whether to assist
Or wait to receive it.

Casting around for a place,
Finally she sits on Golgotha's cold stone.
Where they lay him on her lap
A mother
Receiving her firstborn
But now in searing grief, not in joyful promise.

This moment is last, not first.
The last time she will hold him.
Last time she will see him.
Wanting this closeness to endure,
She lingers, ponders and weeps, alone.
Waiting for consolation she knows will never come.

Men who lifted him down retreat,
Respectfully, in backward steps,
Replaced by sorrow now in giant waves
Accompanied by falling tears
Down from her still youthful face, now worn,
Cascading on flowing garments to the ground.

Behold the man…his body slumped, head back,
Lifeless, spent, displayed across her in death,
Sheer weight releasing yet more anguish,
Remembrance of great promise, now become grim,
She contemplates the piercing sword
Because of him, the rising and falling of many.

Now it really is "finished."
All is quiet like Bethlehem,
Bracketed life cast in serenity.
As she sits, emptied now herself,
Peace seeps unexpectedly down inside
An undisturbed tranquility welcomed in solitude.

She thinks: what is to be, beyond this moment?
Why arise, when I know not where to go,
What to do
Or what the future holds without him?
So she stays and ponders unhurriedly
What eternity's next move might be.

POEMS OF RECOVERY

CAME TO….

I heard that the prodigal son
"Came to his senses,"
That Rip van Winkle woke up
To find America changed,
Himself in a different place.

The "Great Awakening" brought new light
To the darkness in men's souls
As humans came to tree clearings
And open fields
Because their hungry hearts drove them to seek eternal food.

And so I came too…
Came to believe and trust
That God would do what I could not
Yet had so desperately tried…
To fill the empty place, the bottomless and needy pit

Can buckets and barrels with no bottoms
Ever be filled?
Will the self-willed soul ever find rest,
Or will the "waterless places" of worldly drink ever suffice
To slake the heartfelt pangs?

Sanity is what He offered
A better way to think
About myself, Him and others
To reduce inflated ego which saw its bloated bubble
Threatened by a universe of sharpened needles.

Is this possible?
Can my mind find sanity,
Keep Leonardo-like perspective,
And find peaceful pathways? Perhaps.

But first, I must come to believe
That only he can do it.

Lets not get too far down the road,
Nor aim to arrive just yet.
For one thing is asked of me right now
To believe enough to begin
And let go.

CONSCIOUS CONTACT

The defeated ego
Means a difference in prayer
Another path to take
An alternative goal in mind
And a divergent way of living.

Dethroned I sit and wait
Not as before,
When I pursued ambitions, goals, careers
That do nothing
But stoke the fires of me and more.

Now I stop and think
About what he wants
What path he has set before me.
Are there blessings to bestow?
Is there love to show?…Let's wait and see.

No rush…he is creative, imaginative,
This God of the universe.
The One who hides yet speaks
Who makes specific his general will
Incarnates in deeds and words his truth and love.

What is needed other than to enjoy
His presence?
It is to do in kindness
The one blessed thing he has set
Upon human hearts.

For that day only
To respond quietly and invisibly
To the Spirit's urge.

To do and be his servant
In this one time and place, and leave the rest to him.

And then tomorrow
Begin again to seek and find
Like Mary, the best portion,
The simple truth of his love
And of deeds done in mercy and forgiveness.

ECCE HOMO

In a large church
Seated on the aisle
I am quiet, until I see
A man coming toward me,
Supported heavily by another man.

He is crippled, paralyzed on one side,
Face contorted, dragging his body
Slowly, haltingly,
Down the aisle
Toward me.

Slowly, he lifts his gaze
Until his eyes
Remain on mine.
Gradually, I realize
"I know that face and…
We've not seen one another in ages."

So I rise,
Step out of the pew
At the moment his friend
Releases him, and he collapses
Into my arms.

To my great surprise
I am overwhelmed to know
That this man whom I embrace
Is me,
My own crippled self.

When did I forsake you,
Deny and reject you?
When did I send you away

Or dress you up in party clothes
To cover your scars as if this would heal them?

When did I become an enemy
Of my own soul,
And embrace the divided me
Hidden from those I love,
Blocked from the way to paradise?

But now, today, we are reunited
My soul and me,
As I embrace and gaze upon his wounds.
I do not hide his scars,
The dark and ugly secrets
Asking to come to the light.

He who is all love and mercy made us one, my soul and me,
The One who reconciles all things
For his good purpose and mine,
The One who makes whole
That which looks irretrievably broken.

My wounded, crippled self will come
To me again.
But now, I dare not avert my eyes.
Nor let him pass without a warm embrace.
Lest he remain cold, lonely and unredeemed forever.

ENTIRELY READY

Can anyone know
Whence entire readiness derives?
Is it a gift, a mystery?
Or does the will participate,
Cooperating with the plan of the Most High?

"Entirely" is a word
I have not known. Divided has been my will since youth,
Fractured early, cloven between desire
And divine claim and purpose.

Readiness imposed is powerlessness redefined.
It has not worked, nor can.
The rebellious soul is impervious to stone tablets.
Drawn away into its own likes and drives
Lost in the moment's urgency.

So when did my way
Cease to work?
When did I become fed up
With me, and the consequences
Of "entirely not ready" to yield?

The sickness had to run its course.
The pain, sorrow and separation
Must increase as he allowed my disease,
What I craved but could not live with
Nor jettison, to wreck its full havoc on the inner man.

But now, no matter what spirit blows readiness
In my direction,
It has arrived, a gift ready to open and enjoy,
A fact now seen as blessing,
Not deprivation.

Now I ask: when will my brother
Be entirely ready?
When will his surfeit of sickness
Be enough?
To step out on the road to freedom.

I cannot know.
It is not my business but God's.
He who made the human heart,
Eyes, hands and flesh
Will make my brother entirely willing
In his time, not mine.

Until then, I must guard my own heart
And stir up the gift within.
So when my brother is entirely willing,
I will help not hinder,
And we will walk together the road of happy destiny.*

*(From Alcoholics Anonymous)

I WAS WRONG, BACK THEN

I thought I was
Abandoned, bereft, cast-off
By you, my God…beaten and punished
When I was eight, at summer camp,
Lonely, frightened and ashamed.

I thought, back then,
That feelings were facts,
That men were like gods,
Doling out punishment and rewards,
Pain and justice deserved.

I thought parents knew more
Than they did.
How to protect and make
Their children safe,
Free from danger and harm.

But I was wrong, back then,
About God, feelings and parents
Jesus was there, unseen, the suffering servant
Bearing my shame, loneliness and fear.
Standing as a sentinel nearby,
You did not abandon your son.

Now I know… parents are not perfect and feelings are not facts.
No matter how powerful and real they seem.
They must bow to truth.
Men make mistakes, they fall short.
Weak, divided, leaderless are they. *

Parents are fallen and fog-bound,
Hanging on the tiller, at best,
Listening for the bell-buoy, praying against disaster
To avoid the shoals of their own denied short-comings,

Pain and needs.
Almost without knowing, they create room for God to work.

You, O God,
Have leveled the playing field
Under the gaze of your grace.
Altogether broken, we are
All the same redeemed, if willing.

Where are we to take the pieces of our lives,
The shattered and broken dreams?
To you, the vision-giver, the Author of Life.
We come again and again
To find the healing place and eternal rest.

(*Elrond in The Fellowship of the Ring)

IN GIVING WE RECEIVE

Why is it
That I must help others
To be helped,
To ease the pain in another man's soul
To heal my own?

Is this the way
God set it up to be?
That it is our troubles and problems
Which bind us together in the bundle of life
Like nothing else can?

Experience concurs.
When I am thirsty
Or peckish and unstable
I often find relief in doing for others
What I myself desire.

This is the only thing
That stills the insistent voice of "more" and "better."
To reach down not up,
To the lonely, wounded and needy
With the helping hand of time spent.

The truth is that my yearning soul
Is only quieted
When my actions become
The Balm of Gilead, the affirming hand
To the heart of another.

I must re-cross Jordan
To the land from which I came,
Carrying its thirst-quenching waters
To that weary place
Of threatened and fading hope in a single human heart.

Only when he is satiated
Can my soul be restored
When his burden is laid down,
I feel refreshed and behold life in its wholeness,
Not in the desperate particularity of desire.

Did the "good" Samaritan
Find his inferiority healed by tending to another,
Going beyond the call of duty
To care for the man beaten by thieves
And left for dead?

We are not told.
But this I know.
It is in healing that we are healed.
It is in giving that we receive.
It is in pardoning that we are pardoned.*

For I am learning this life lesson.
The separateness of you and me has its limits
Beyond what makes us different
Dwells something higher
Which binds us all together
And ties our destinies in an eternal, unbreakable knot.

*(The Prayer of St. Francis)

MAKING AMENDS

Times past
When harm done to others
Was my right and blind entitlement.
I thought nothing of just "moving on,"
Running through the thistles of threatening awareness.

Laughing, crying were immaterial
To my destructive direction
On which I refused to gaze,
Register and comprehend.
Connected dots of misdeeds remained scattered,
Patterns unrecognized.

We all make mistakes
Look back
And cringe at what we did and said.
Could that really have happened?
Was I really that self-centered,
Desperate and wounding?

So now the facing comes
The moment to begin to mend inflicted pain.
Where do I start?
What do I say? Whom do I contact first?
Swirling thoughts make clouded intentions
Only time will clarify.

So I cannot hurry
This sorting out process
Of imagined and actual wrongs,
The specter of rejection's fears
Coming to annihilate good intentions and inevitable steps.

All I do now
Is make a list…write down names

Perform a scan of the past looking for cracks
Dark places, relational pain,
Hurricane force neediness run amok,
To begin my healing plan.

Just to be willing is the start.
To desire the wrongs set right and acknowledge wounds
I must release upstream the closed up flood of denial
To flow naturally downhill
Toward the plain of reconciliation, the leveling place.

The time to act and speak is not yet,
For awareness must come first,
Accompanied by concrete events and names.
Instinctively I will know when to step out,
And when to wait, lest others be further wounded.

Not all should be ventured soon,
Nor contact hurried in frenzied pace.
I must wait for His time and place
And know how to speak and what
Lest desperate dumping spoil the plan.

One fact emerges
With clarity and purpose
Beyond all others.
I am willing to put it right
And that is enough.

POWERLESS

When did my momentary lapse
Become rut-like reality?
When did the stumble
Become the fall,
The sin emerge as character flaw?

Was there a time
When I could have turned back
Straightened up and brushed my clothes
And returned to the path for good
Without memory or care of why I strayed?

Or was I captured the very first time
By chemicals intoxicating the brain
The delicious mix of pleasure, power and privacy
Stirring the cocktail inside my head
Into a godlike trance?

The one true God knows
But one thing I know also.
I am here today, powerless
Over this, the wave that has overwhelmed me,
And flooded my ship of fools
With fellow travelers beside.

Shipwrecked, clinging to the rocks
I now know
There is neither health nor help in me
In the "I" now captive
To this fallen force that wants the whole of me.

And so....I begin again
Admitting the magnificent defeat he engineered,
The only hope for freedom
To accept a new beginning.

If there is to be one,
Let it begin here.

And where is here?
The place where the excuses, blaming
Schemes, bargains and secrecy
Stop...for one simple reason.
They have all conspired to lead me
To this intolerable place of pain.

So finally, powerless and ready
I take another path
His way...the only possible way
To health, humanity and community.
And so I let go
And let Him begin the rescue he planned all along.

RUB AND THE ROAD

Now comes the rub.
The moment of decision arrives.
Do I, can I, live without
The drivers of my dis-ease,
Flaws that draw me back to the place of pain?

Devils mock, secularists deride.
What a joke!
Become different? At your age?
Living without the stuff? Ha!
Has Linus ever tossed away the blanket permanently never to pick it
up again?

All that comes before is excavation for this.
The crater exists only to be filled
In the prayerful request
The audacious yet quiet petition
To take it away,
Finally, fully and forever.

So what if it takes a while.
Never mind that other defects lie behind
The rock just prayerfully removed.
This is progress, not perfection,
Real, incremental change, insides opened to the healing breeze.

Why did I doubt this before?
Why did I make such feeble excuses?
Was I unwilling to let go completely?
Was I a believer, unbelieving?
Yes, all of this and more.

Any excuse covers a tsunami
Of unwilling urges flooding the soul.

There are reasons galore
Why I sought to blend with fallen man,
Hiding in Eden's forest hoping not to be found.

What messenger could break through to reach
My soul's blind eyes?
What reality could dispel fantasies
Of self-sufficiency, false safety, and delusion?
What unwelcome guest approached my door?

Ah....God's most useful servant found me out,
Searing, private pain came as clarion call to "let go absolutely."
Humanity, though it shared my lot
Never knocked with help... why should they?
The unready have no message, nor consolation, for the recently
willing.

No, it took the ring of fellowship
To turn the trail of tears to freedom's way.
Walking patiently with me down the well-worn path
To the willing place where I arrived today,
The new residence of asking.

And what is the petition?
"Take it away", slowly, quickly, does not matter.
"Remove," at whatever pace is needed
But please remove my shortcomings,
Eliminate the flaws that draw me
Away from you and others.

Take all of me good and bad
Remove every defect
Make me useful to you and others
Grant me strength to do your bidding.
A simple prayer and yet... now the work of a lifetime begins.

SEARCHING AND FEARLESS

Do I dare look inside
At the actual me,
Words and actions, thoughts and deeds
Perpetrated in this world, written in the record?
Will I examine my soul's sewage in the detail?

What can be the purpose
Of looking within
And seeing the truth
That is the historical me
The man who is, not him who would be.

Searching means the light
Must probe into every nook
To the corners and hidden places
That lie in dank darkness,
Resting rotten and undisturbed
By the light of truth and honesty.

What might I find? I fear to look and not to,
But I will not know until I gaze
With fearless eyes at the fallen fellow become me,
The wounded warrior whose arrows
Have pieced his own soul and others.

In looking, now I see the man who would change
Must release the clinging ashes
Of his tarnished self all wrapped in dusty defects
No longer useful or helpful or desired
For the freedom walk that lies ahead.

And so I take the quiet careful inventory,
Open the catalog and record them
One by one, each by name

Bitter, troubled thoughts, evil deeds
Broken promises, slowly, right to the last one.

I must gaze at this picture for a time
Full frontal, in all its hideous truth.
But surprise to me, in looking the letting go begins.
The man who was slips off his shackles
The man who will be begins to begin.

I dare not move on too quickly
Until the probing Light has swept my soul's house,
The work now completed.
Having looked, now I can tell another human
Who I really am and begin to be both another and myself.

THE GODDESS OF DENIAL

She came to me
Long ago
In a youthful life
In my time of woe
And took up residence nearby.

She promised when I was weak
When I felt a little shame
When things went wrong
And I felt the hunger pang
That she would fix me quick and nullify the pain.

Her throne beguiling
Her raiment bewitching
She whispered soft and said
"No one needs to know but you and me."
Never mentioning the dread.

And so our convenient swap began
As I used her and she me
I to get relief
She to extend her reach
Into human hearts, her place of restless rest.

But soon her meager bread
Became too little for peckish me.
"I want more," I said
"I am still hungry, though I eat your fare.
I want meat to fill my head with more,
To take this load of dread."

And so she gave and so I took
Unquestioning I ate the hook and swallowed
Never thinking the fisherman, now the fish
The hunter now the meal.

The free man now dead to freedom,
The found now lost again.

My goddess from beginning
Never told the real price
The cost of that first purchase and her expanding sale of goods.
That if I unrelentingly consumed
Would cost me all....I never understood.

I now in panic asked "Why did you lie?"
Why was not the price disclosed?"
My goddess laughed to me and said,
"I always lie, that is my trade and all of man like you
Still talk to me and take my wares unthinkingly
As long as time will last."

So when you turn to her
And demand delivery from your time of trial
Remember that her name comes earned, my goddess of denial.
She never, ever tells the truth while pouring out her vial
Of things that please, if only for a moment,
While their fruit abides a while.

Her trade is fixed for one large goal
So permanent, so long
To take the soul of man and bind it to her throne.
And there to do her bidding, while life shall last
While man despairs of future and of past.

So if you think you'll win
At her ancient game
Remember that the she's holding all the cards,
And knows them all by name.
My goddess of denial knows that if with her you play,
She will own what should be God's
And in this life you'll pay.

(With thanks to "Jamie" wherever he may be)

46

THE SPIRIT KILLS...
THE LETTER GIVES LIFE

Generalities are useless to the soul.
Rigorous exactitude must win the day, or I gain nothing,
As I pour over my life's wreckage
Like an NTSB researcher
After the plane went down.

Why did I lose altitude?
What does the debris tell me
Of why I went off course?
What does the black box recording show
Of last words before the crash?

Oh blessed particularity of demise!
Oh liberating truth of what I did and why.
To another human being I must go or remain
Below the radar, invisible, unknown.
Confessor, friend, listening one…you will hear the man that no one knows,
The unvarnished record of deeds both good and evil.

"Search me and know me, O God
And see if there be any wicked way within me."
To adumbrate the record of wrongs,
To write and speak with stark specificity to another soul
Is the end of secrecy, the beginning of redemption.

At this moment I cease to stand apart, alone, self-abandoned.
I join openly the fallen race of men,
Free from pretension, minimizing and self-loathing,
And begin to walk the pathway to sanity,
To wholeness, human community and God himself.

I cannot go to God whom I have not seen

Unless I can go to my brother whom I have seen.
Nor can I be real with a heavenly God
And unreal with my earthly brother who, like me,
Must be known and loved as he is, or not at all.

My story tumbles out and another gathers in the real, the specific me.
He accepts the truth my separated soul has longed to hear.
I am a mixture like the rest of humanity.
The truth I have hitherto avoided at all cost is this:
I am normal, fallen, loved and redeemed.

Now God gives a gift, a companion for the journey
Who enters my life.
Heaven sent to me, in this sense.
Having heard the facts of my existence, I now know convincingly,
I am not alone.

TURNING IT OVER

The question in turning over
Is to whom
Am I giving control?
What person will now take possession
Where I have miserably failed?

Is there someone worthy
To be captain of my "unconquerable" soul,* I laugh?
Now dominated, the once free man now enslaved,
This captain, who steered the ship
Upon the rocks in ruin, yet still protests his navigational excellence?

("Invictus" by William Ernest Henley)

Will it be my neighbor,
My friend in whom I trust?
Yet he of similar a fate, now broken
Can only point the way
Beyond himself to you.

No, the full handing over
Can only be given to the untainted,
All knowing and loving Power
Who takes hunger and the wounds
And bears them all away
To begin new life in me.

Yet my understanding of you is partial
Your name barely lit upon the page
And within my breast.
I had heard of you but not known your power
Nor invoked your name in the quagmire of my youth.

This "God of my understanding" meets me
In the place I can walk in a few hours pace

He does not ask a journey to the heights
But meets me in the foothills
And takes my hand.

To where have I come today?
Just one more step now to a decision
To turn it over, my life,
My self to a future yet unknown
For one thing I know beyond any question
To keep this life of mine to myself is failure guaranteed.

And so I place my hand in his
And surrender,
Knowing that tomorrow
I must do the same again
To live the life he gives.

WHY IT IS ALWAYS MY FAULT

When I am disturbed
By the slight, the sidelong comment,
Criticism or success of another,
I have learned
That this is always my fault…always.

This is God's nudge
His whispered word in my ear,
The divine alert to approaching danger
That could derail the train of progress
Of connection with God and man.

Oh, the felix culpa, this happy fault
To finally understand revealed truth
That others may indulge their righteous anger
Free to confront the evil
Outside themselves.

But I cannot.
I must not entertain the delusion
Of nonexistent righteousness and moral purity
That I do not possess
Even a little.

And so, I must be vigilant when wronged
When ego is diminished
By inevitable happenings as I walk toward heaven,
And the inner wound detector
Registers the pain.

The one thing I cannot do is simple,
To focus on outside snubs
Or affronts to the inner man.
When the wounded man is indulged and pitied,
Justification waits at my soul's door to have his way.

So let the innocent and pure vent their anger
Toward unrighteous others.
But I, the tainted, must look inside
To find and name the reason
For the truth about the inner me
And discover a better path ahead, the path of progress and peace.

WILLINGNESS

How can I repair
The torn garments of other's lives
The burning, wounding words and deeds
That stoked the fire
Of my deceit and harm?

Unconscious of the damage then
Because of inflated self,
Now I see the wreckage
Have surveyed the chaotic scene
Where self unrestrained wrecked havoc on another soul.

What can I say or do?
Can the broken be made whole again?
Can the wounder assist the wounded
In healing or the wounded receive from him
Who caused the pain?

Worse, may further pain
Be inflicted in desperate attempt
To close the original?
This one thing I cannot do
Nor allow.... to inflict blow on blow to exacerbate what I once
caused.

Great caution here is needed
To know the time and manner
The way and place to make amends,
Or stay away lest further pain
Be caused or unwanted contact materialize in unsought moments.

The best amends is a changed life
Well lived with kindness

Thoughts and prayers for others
Giving not taking when the insistent voice
Of addiction is stilled with the quietness of love.

Without a clear path,
I wait to find direction
The willingness in making right.
God gives me all the time I need
Until the coast is clear to act and make amends.

Until then, I wait and give Him room,
My willingness to make it right
To admit my wrong and ask forgiveness
For all the hurts I have caused
To remain free one day at a time.

POEMS OF LIFE

CHRISTMAS FOR THE AGES

Deep in winter.
Darkness seeps into our bones
In the midst of cold
We await the warmth of God's tiny light,
Struggling to be born.

A new beginning for the ages.
A baby, no, a man for all time.
Against all odds,
Against the decline of human history
Against the darkness seeking his demise.

Then suddenly, he is born. Christ is born today,
Collapsing every Christmas in human history
In our lives and memory
Into this Christmas, this eternal now,
Asking entrance once again.

Today he comes in stillness and night,
Bearing unseen gifts of grace and truth, what we need but dare not
ask.
Many will never unwrap them nor have eyes to behold.
But some unexpectedly, suddenly, like the shepherds of old,
Will see the glory all around and worship at his feet.

He asks: Give me your gift, your darkness, your unreachable place of
pain.
Conflicted memories of Christmases past?
Rejection, isolation, broken dreams, vain wishes?
Never mind. He comes to take these and more, to redeem it all,
And will.

The human soul cries out: Can he do it for me?
He did. He has. He will… and he gives new life, the greatest gift of all.
But be still. Be quiet. He comes again in the vacant spaces of our souls
Seeking Bethlehem's birth in us.
Again.

60

MAINE AT DAWN

On Maine's rocky coast
Slowly at dawn
An hour before I see the sun
Light rises
Fanfare to a new day

In the place
Where land, sea and sky converge
I wait the dawning
Of God's new day
Expectantly with childlike wonder

Sky brightens, turns gently blue
Gulls float upward and fly
To who knows where.
Others follow
As if by pre-arranged meeting

The sun rises in power and light
First red, then orange and amber
Finally unwatchable yellow
Ever ascending
The bridegroom coming forth from his chamber*

*(Psalm 19)

On cue
The sea calms and wind subsides
Waves lie down, reassured and overseen
By dawn's emerging warmth and light

My soul too, a little sleepless
Wondering, beseeching, forward leaning
Finds rest and hope.
The light of God's presence comes
Calling me to reflect and enjoy his glory this day.

MICHELANGELO'S DAVID

The crown of youth
And Renaissance man,
He stands poised, wary, alert
Vision cast across the valley
Ready for life-defining battle, improbable victory.

He knows
Neither the outrages
Nor the ennui of power yet to come,
It's inability to fill his empty soul,
Nor its certainty in revealing it.

Middle age, moral decay
The loss of a child
The betrayal of another
On this day, none is hinted at
Nor even imagined.

Dark days running from Saul,
The remembrance of spear barely dodged,
Anointed yet despised,
Cave-dwelling with band of brothers
Living years in the not-yet kingship.

All is yet to come,
Yet to be suffered, wondered at, endured
In a future life
Of triumph and troubles, hot tears, repentance
And restoration of the heart once wholly God's.

Likewise, Renaissance man,
Embodied in him,
Could not foresee Savonarola,
Botticelli burning paintings in the street
Man killing man for religion.

Nor could David's masterful creator
And flowering Florence possibly know
That agony would mix with ecstacy*
Poverty with riches
And servitude with liberty in the steps of time.

But for this David,
Today is pure unblemished vistas
Of courage risking all
And a future of renown
Awaiting him in the Valley of Elah.

As we age, in the memory of youthful daring
And the God who made us so,
We will find the seeds
Of what we will be again
In another, unfallen world.

*(The Agony and the Ecstasy by Irving Stone)

SITTING WITH JOB

When Job suffered greatly
Beyond comprehension
His friends came and sat with him in the dust
In silence, for seven days
Saying nothing.

If only they had continued
To sit quietly
With their anguished friend
As companions
To his lonely soul.

If only they could admit
Their powerlessness over his wounds
And embrace their own inability and weakness
If only they had waited and silently prayed and watched
To see what God would do.

Instead, they became miserable comforters,
Multiplying words upon words,
Weaving man-made causes for Job's pain
With reasons, not help,
To placate themselves, not Job.

Too bad Job's friends left him too soon.
Too bad they were not witnesses
To God's restoration of their friend
In God's way, received in patience,
In God's time.

When I am in pain and anguish
Much less than Job's, though mine,
Troubling and often enduring
With little relief, answers or deliverance
Accompanied by enigmas I cannot solve,

Will you just sit with me
In silence?
So I will know I am not alone
Can you forswear your own answers
So we can wait together for God's?

It may take a while.
Maybe more than seven days.
But I need more than a text
Or an online meeting.
I need you to wait for God with me,
Until He comes in power.

This is not
Just what I need.
It is what the world needs, right now.
May we not be in such a hurry
That we miss the time it takes to find hope.

THE AGE OF NOT KNOWING

How do I know
What I do not know
At this time in my life
When compasses, calendars and watches
And people fail to guide
Or tell me where I am or should be?

Or do I already know
And am using other's diffidence
As an excuse?
You would think that at my age
I would be more confident where my path lies, but I am not.

We spend our lives
On a track of working, striving and climbing
Believing that tomorrow and next week
There are projects, people and plans
That resemble a life-pattern, cocktail party reciprocity.

But does God care that I do not know
What I should know
About these things?
Or is He acting on a different plane altogether,
Sitting loose to my worldly hopes and dreams?

I guess Jesus really meant "seek ye first…"
Yet my mind wanders back to food, shelter, clothing
Jobs, paystubs, taxes, 401ks and health and life insurance.
But not for long… soon more of my last things enter my mind,
And His "first things" shine forth again.

Could it be that these "not knowing" years
Are meant to loosen me
From this world? (Hebrews 11)

Are they crafted just so I know that the important things
Are dawning just as my worldly sun begins to set?

If that is so, I want to embrace this place,
Because it just may be that God is here
And Like Jacob, "I knew it not,"
Beckoning me to come to Him,
Like Jesus to Peter on the waves,
To be free and to believe, not in the sunshine
But in the stormy cloud of unknowing where He dwells in eternal
light.

WAITING FOR GOD

The difference between You and me,
My God,
Is that I must learn to wait…..

For things to move
For problems resolving as I see them
For the answers to my prayers
Or prayers conforming to my answers.

You must like us humans to wait,
Because we do it….a lot.
Bewildered, living in the dust,
We wait and sigh and pray and wait some more,
Wondering if it is doing any good.

Is this to build our character?
Is it to build our faith?
Or to delight in the answer still more
When it comes in unexpected ways,
From unknown sources that could not know our need
Or from others that knew and acted,
So we are certain it could only be You that made provision?

Is this your delight?
O hidden God,
Is this your playful dance with humankind,
That walks with us through the valley
But is rarely eager to reveal the way
Out of it to the mountain of vision
Lest we say we do not need you as we once did?

Perhaps you know us too well
Our rebellious prideful spirit
That says, "All will be well, without him.

I can manage, succeed and find the cool springs
Without his help."

The one thing you never do, my God, is wait
One time is as another to you
Our lives all Now
Unfolded before you, as a canvas not hidden,
Not dark and unknown as our murky vision sees
To you the Father of Lights
Who knows all things.

Here is what I have come to know
About waiting,
Which I despise and reject without knowledge
And tests my soul as nothing else
Until I find my answer.

All things in my life…all things
Conspire to drive me to you,
Including waiting.
All roads in my life are leading me
To you….therefore I have learned
That you are the destination
Not my answer that I so desperately seek.

So I will sit loose to "answers."
Because you are my goal, my destination,
Not some thing apart from your presence,
That I so easily put in your place
As my highest good. When I know this,
I become a little more like You
And am at peace.

FEET OF DESTINY

Our feet
Are the lowest part
Of our human bodies
They keep us grounded
Propel us along our God-given path
Giving us a grip on the world

But…they are liable to stumble
To slip, to cause us to fall headlong
When walking on rocky, unfamiliar
And sometimes forbidden soil
Not easily traversed without trouble.

Your word is a lamp unto our feet
And a light upon our path
May we walk in the light
Of your presence, O God
Without stumbling.

O God, You have "preserved our lives
And kept our feet from slipping."
"You have delivered me from death
And my feet from stumbling."
Make level paths for my feet, O my God

Beautiful feet…of the one
Who brings good news.
You brought those feet to me
Proclaiming peace, good tidings,
Salvation to one who wandered from the path.

Feet of ministry…the head cannot say
"I do not need you"….I am higher
And more heavenly than you. No,

The head can do nothing
Unless the feet agree to go.

Jesus's feet, that trudged the roads
Of Palestine accompanied by fallen feet
Yet, it was he who washed theirs
With objection
"Lord, you will never….!"

The feet of rejection…
If they do not receive you,
Cast off the dust from you feet
Don't stay…keep moving forward
Til you find a house of peace.

Precious feet…on the cross…
"They have pierced my hands and my feet"
Somehow they provide the last pedestal for earthly life
Bloody, yet providing support
As still he clings to life

Resurrection feet…with Mary
Clinging to those feet
She worships
"Do not hold me.
For I have not yet ascended…."

Victorious feet…everything that exists
Will be under them. Satan crushed
Beneath them…the feet of bronze
Glowing in a furnace
The One beheld in awe and power.

To Him who is able
To prevent us from falling
Or, when having fallen, picks us up
And will never let us go
To Him be the glory, forever. Amen

A FINAL WORD:
SEEDS OF HOPE

A couple of years ago, my 87 year old mother and I conducted several errands and stops in the car during the day while I visited her in Maine. I was a little annoyed when she said, "I just want to do one more thing before we go home. I want to go to Thornton Oaks (her assisted living new home where she was moving in a month) and plant some bulbs in the garden for next spring." So being a captive travelling companion, I agreed. When we arrived, I unloaded her special kneeler equipped with handles she uses to plant things and took it to the small garden outside her future unit and set it in the midst of the garden. There I watched her slowly kneel down, open her small package of crocus bulbs, and with her aging hands patiently plant them in the ground in clusters of five. Then she placed those hands on the kneeler handles and slowly and shakily raised her aching knees off the ground.

As I watched her, I said to myself. She's not planting bulbs. She's planting hope. (Her name is Hope.) Shortly thereafter, I returned to our church in Jacksonville, which was moving to new location. When I arrived at our dedication service, I was bowled over by the words chosen for the occasion.

[1] The desert and the parched land will be glad;
    the wilderness will rejoice and blossom.
    Like the crocus, [2] it will burst into bloom;
    it will rejoice greatly and shout for joy.
    The glory of Lebanon will be given to it,
    the splendor of Carmel and Sharon;

they will see the glory of the LORD,
the splendor of our God.
³ Strengthen the feeble hands,
steady the knees that give way;

⁴ say to those with fearful hearts,
"Be strong, do not fear;
your God will come,
he will come with vengeance;
with divine retribution
he will come to save you." Isaiah 35:1-4

God truly knows our lying down, our rising up and all the hairs on our head. He is continually planting seeds of hope within us. "May the God of hope fill (us) with all joy and peace in believing through the power of the Holy Spirit." Romans 15:13.

Made in the USA
Middletown, DE
23 September 2021